Chapter 4: President Clinton

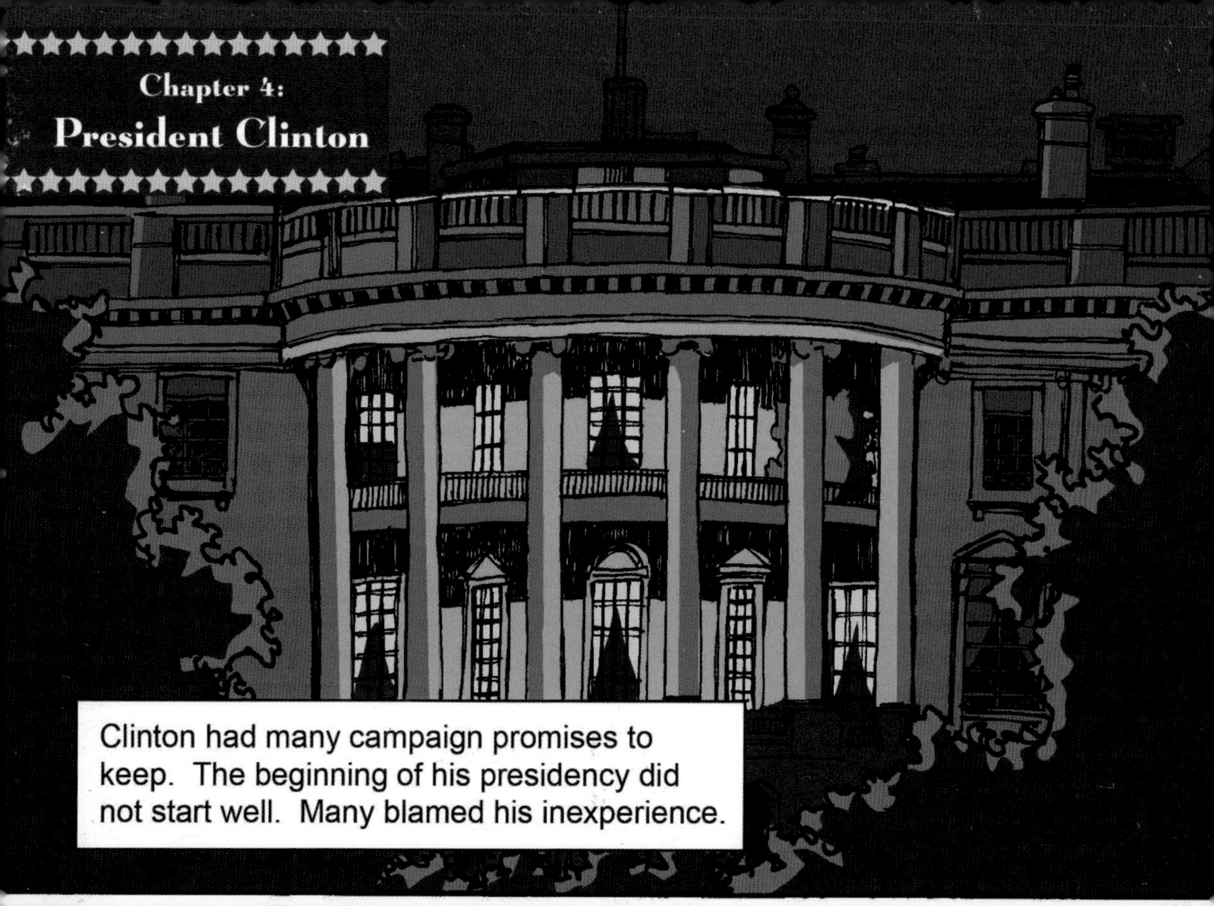
Clinton had many campaign promises to keep. The beginning of his presidency did not start well. Many blamed his inexperience.

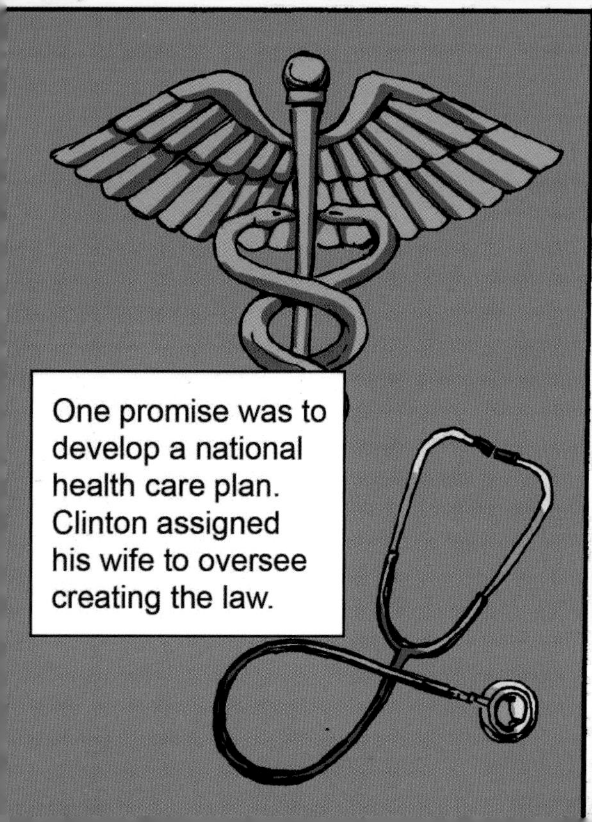
One promise was to develop a national health care plan. Clinton assigned his wife to oversee creating the law.

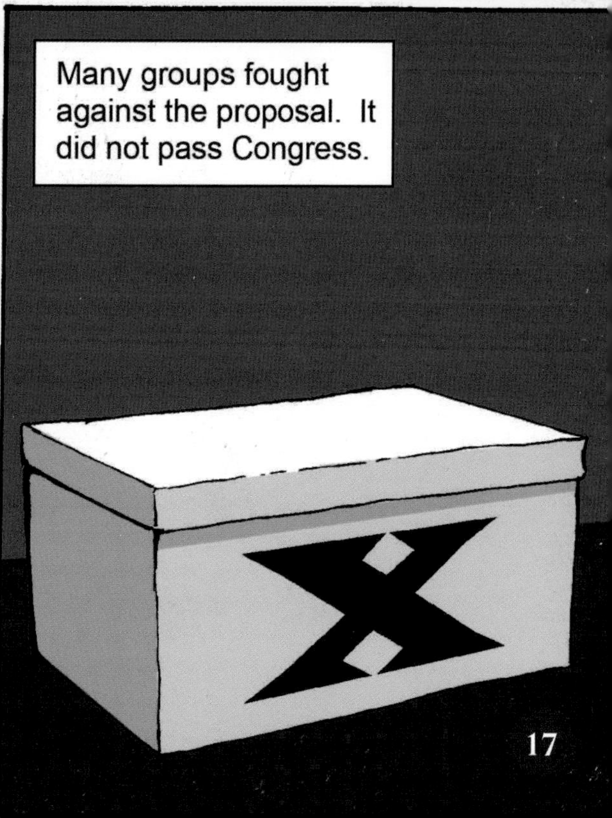
Many groups fought against the proposal. It did not pass Congress.

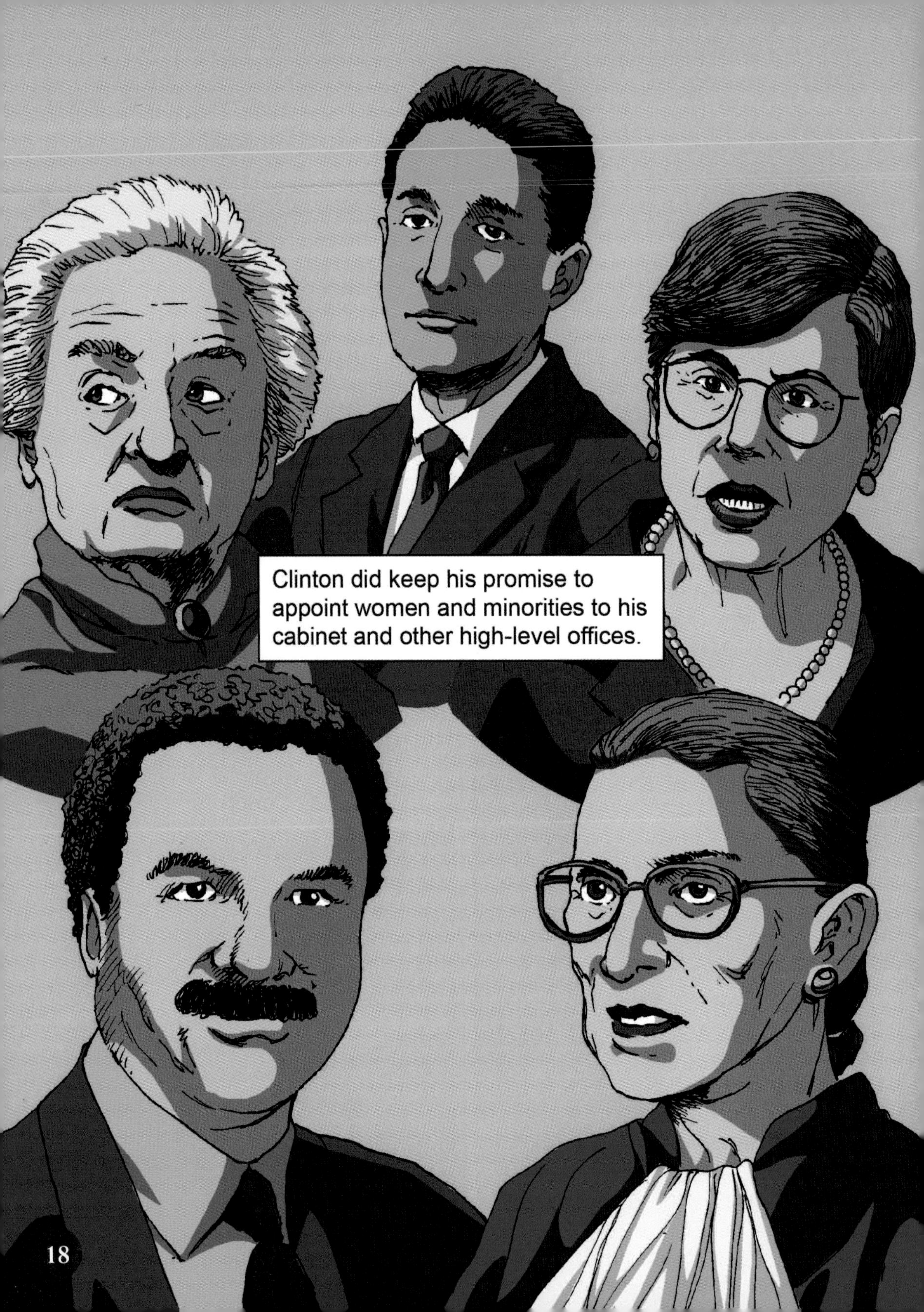
Clinton did keep his promise to appoint women and minorities to his cabinet and other high-level offices.

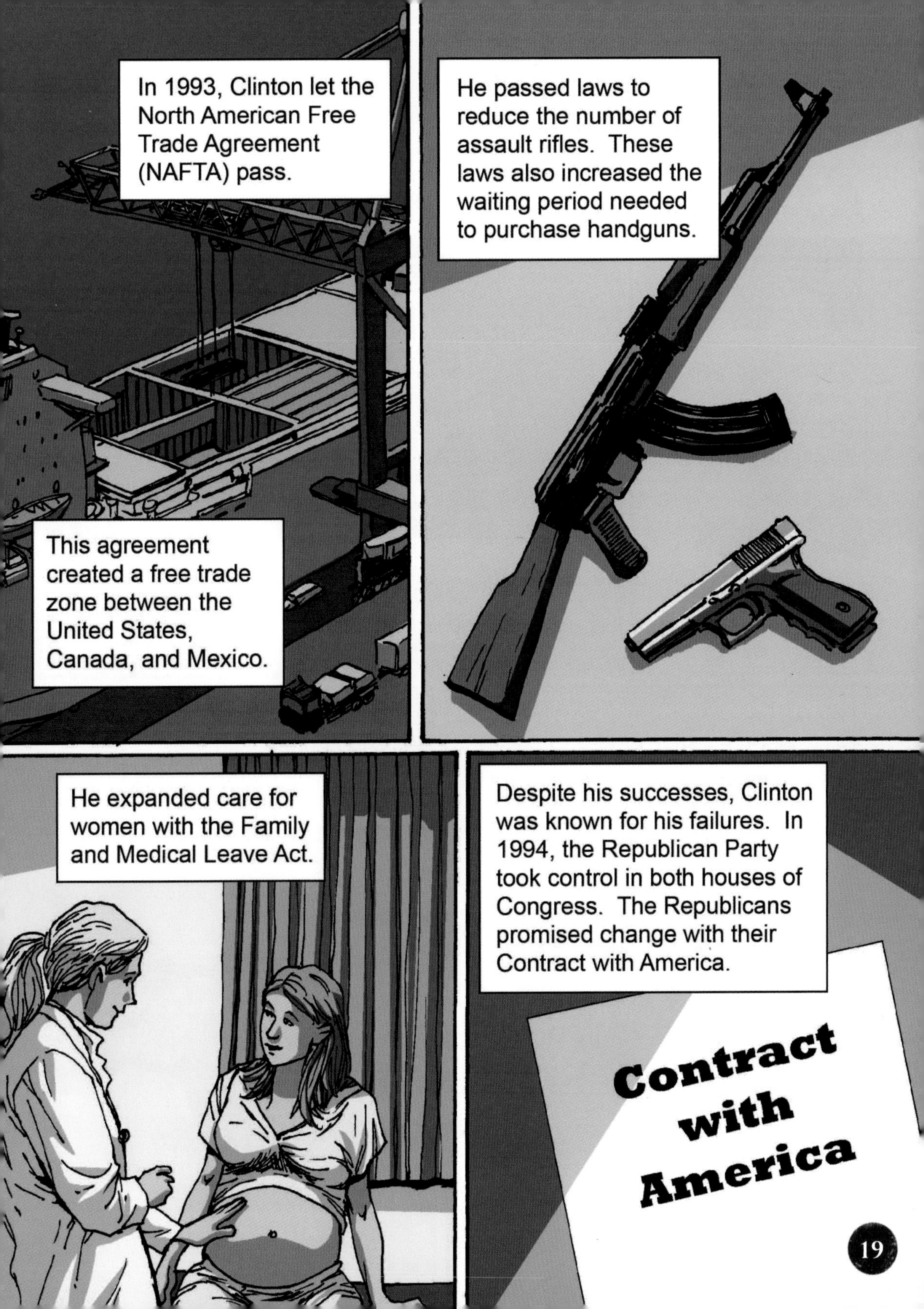
In 1993, Clinton let the North American Free Trade Agreement (NAFTA) pass.
This agreement created a free trade zone between the United States, Canada, and Mexico.
He passed laws to reduce the number of assault rifles. These laws also increased the waiting period needed to purchase handguns.
He expanded care for women with the Family and Medical Leave Act.
Despite his successes, Clinton was known for his failures. In 1994, the Republican Party took control in both houses of Congress. The Republicans promised change with their Contract with America.
Contract with America

Chapter 5: A Second Term

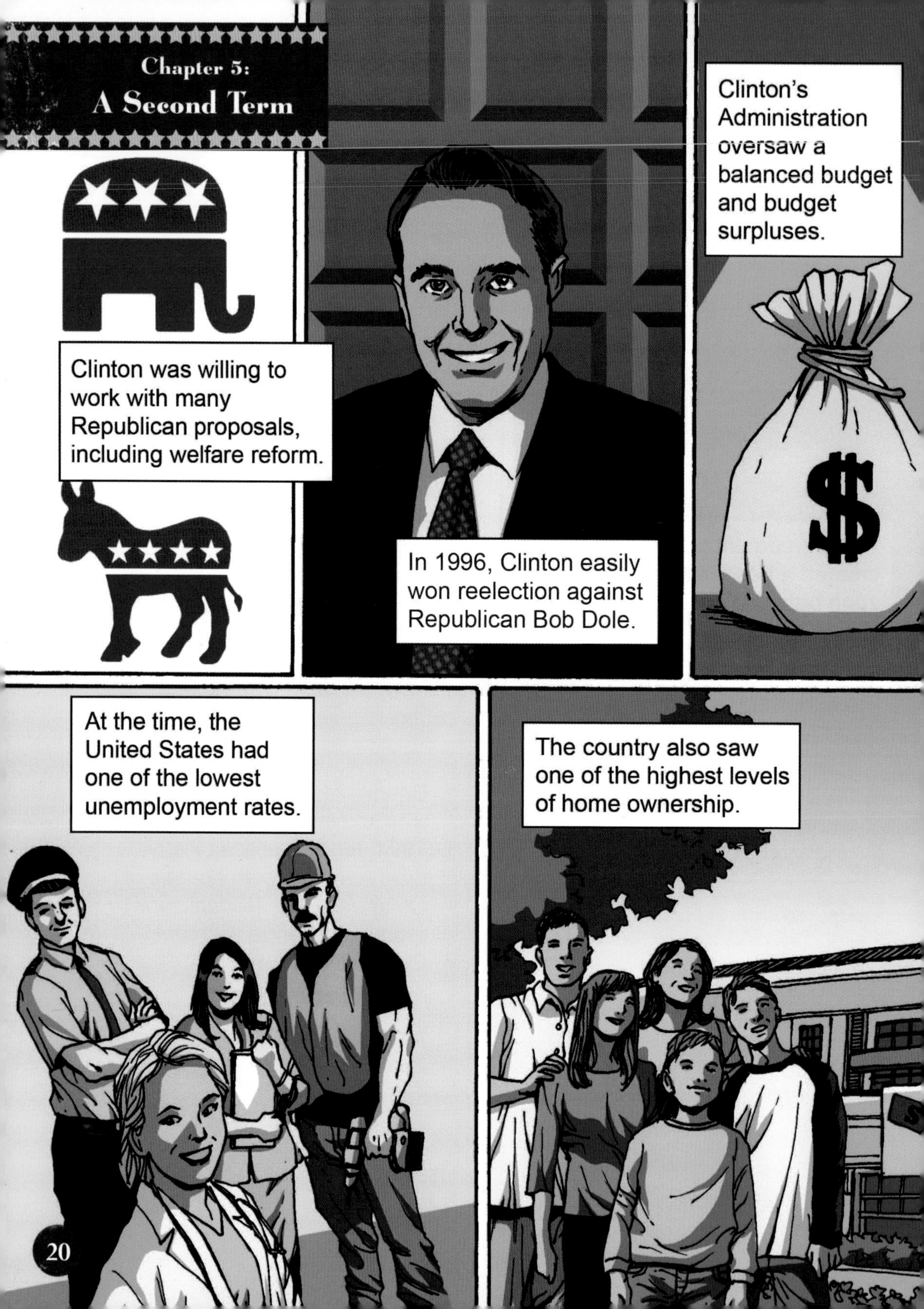
Clinton was willing to work with many Republican proposals, including welfare reform.
In 1996, Clinton easily won reelection against Republican Bob Dole.
Clinton's Administration oversaw a balanced budget and budget surpluses.
$
At the time, the United States had one of the lowest unemployment rates.
The country also saw one of the highest levels of home ownership.

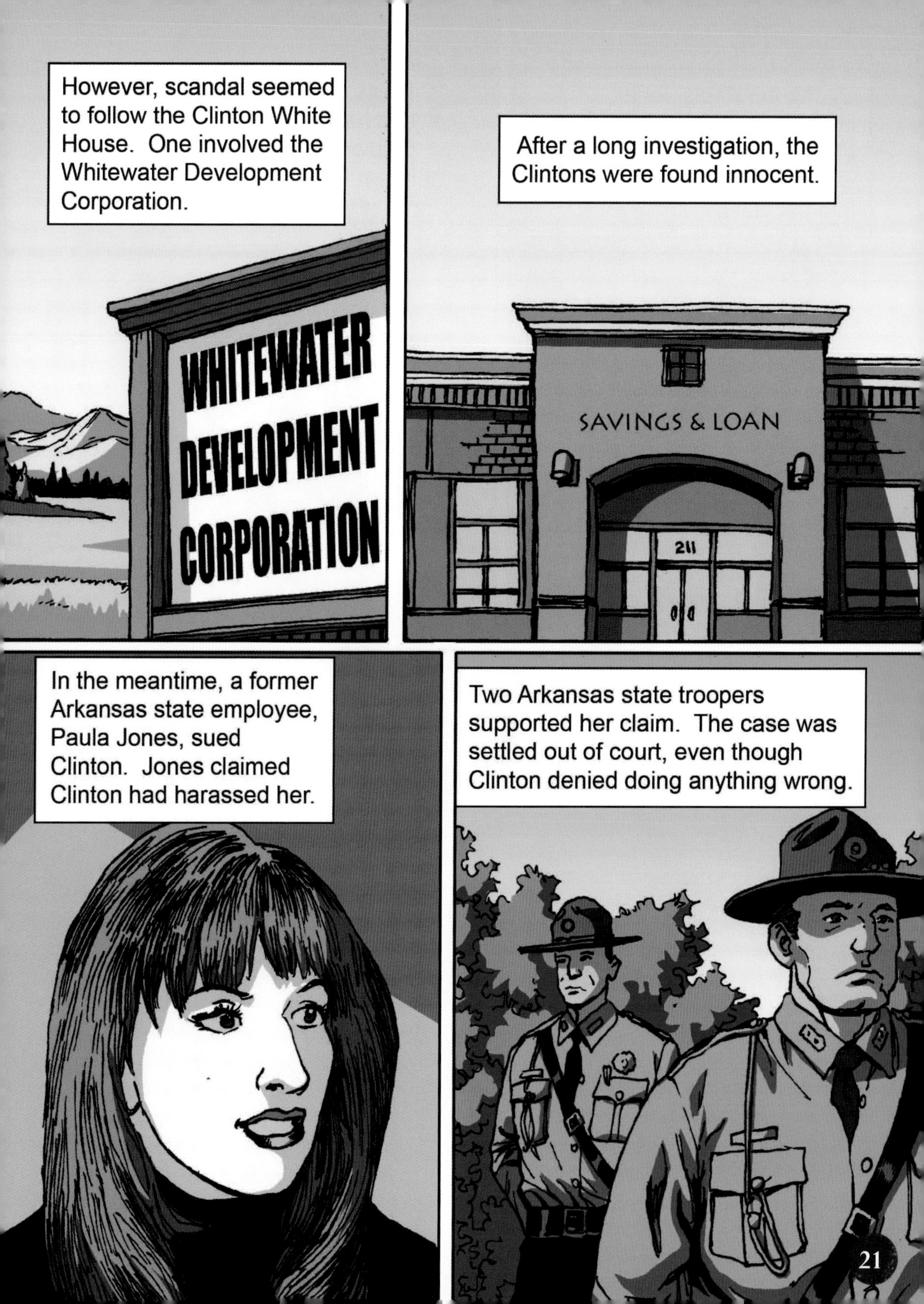
However, scandal seemed to follow the Clinton White House. One involved the Whitewater Development Corporation.
WHITEWATER DEVELOPMENT CORPORATION
After a long investigation, the Clintons were found innocent.
SAVINGS & LOAN
211
In the meantime, a former Arkansas state employee, Paula Jones, sued Clinton. Jones claimed Clinton had harassed her.
Two Arkansas state troopers supported her claim. The case was settled out of court, even though Clinton denied doing anything wrong.

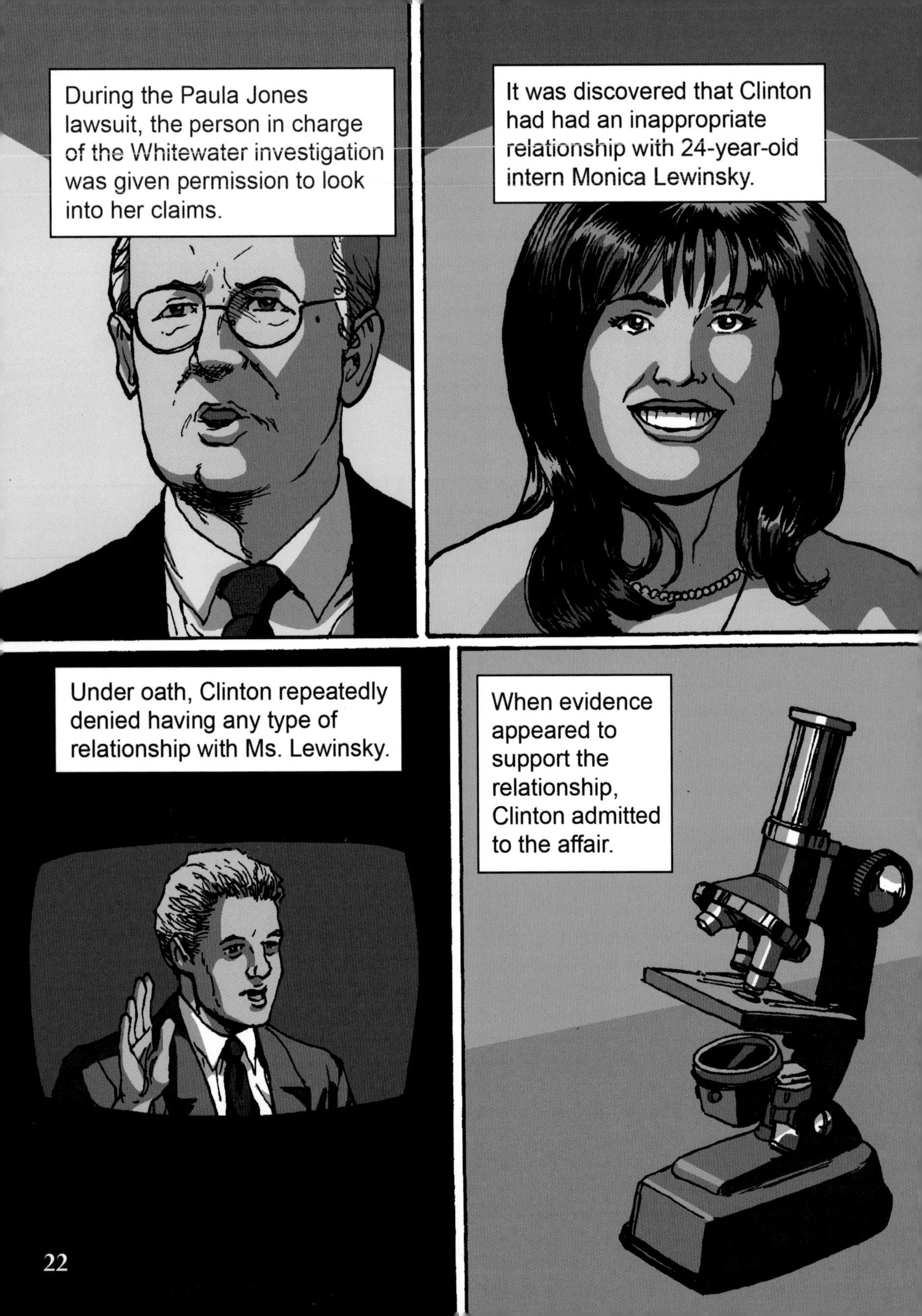
During the Paula Jones lawsuit, the person in charge of the Whitewater investigation was given permission to look into her claims.
It was discovered that Clinton had had an inappropriate relationship with 24-year-old intern Monica Lewinsky.
Under oath, Clinton repeatedly denied having any type of relationship with Ms. Lewinsky.
When evidence appeared to support the relationship, Clinton admitted to the affair.

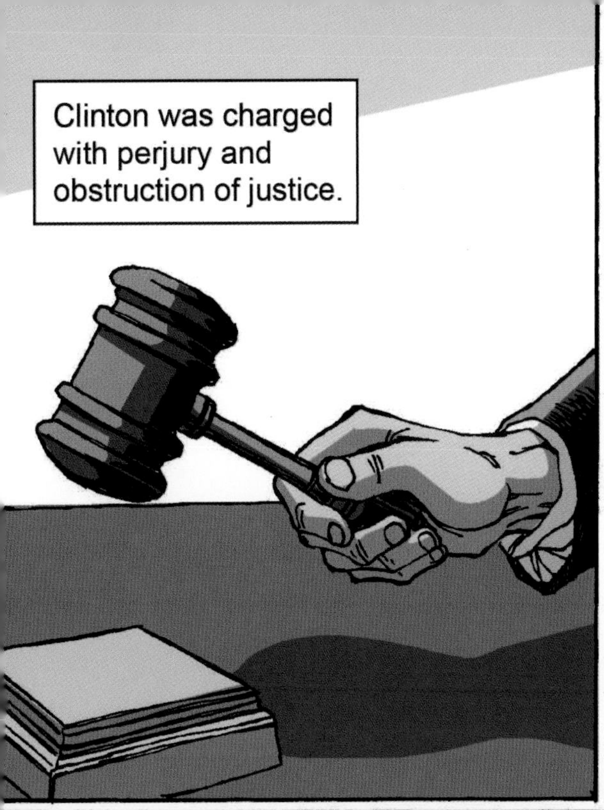
Clinton was charged with perjury and obstruction of justice.

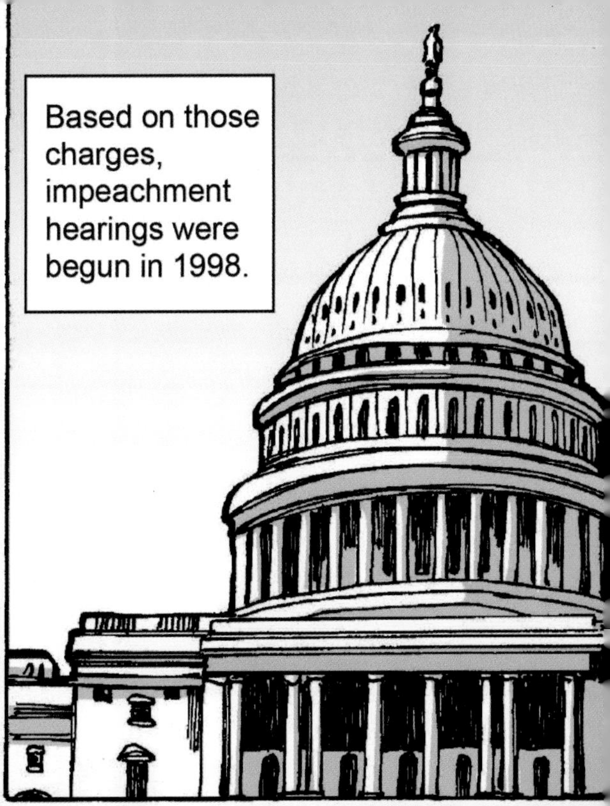
Based on those charges, impeachment hearings were begun in 1998.

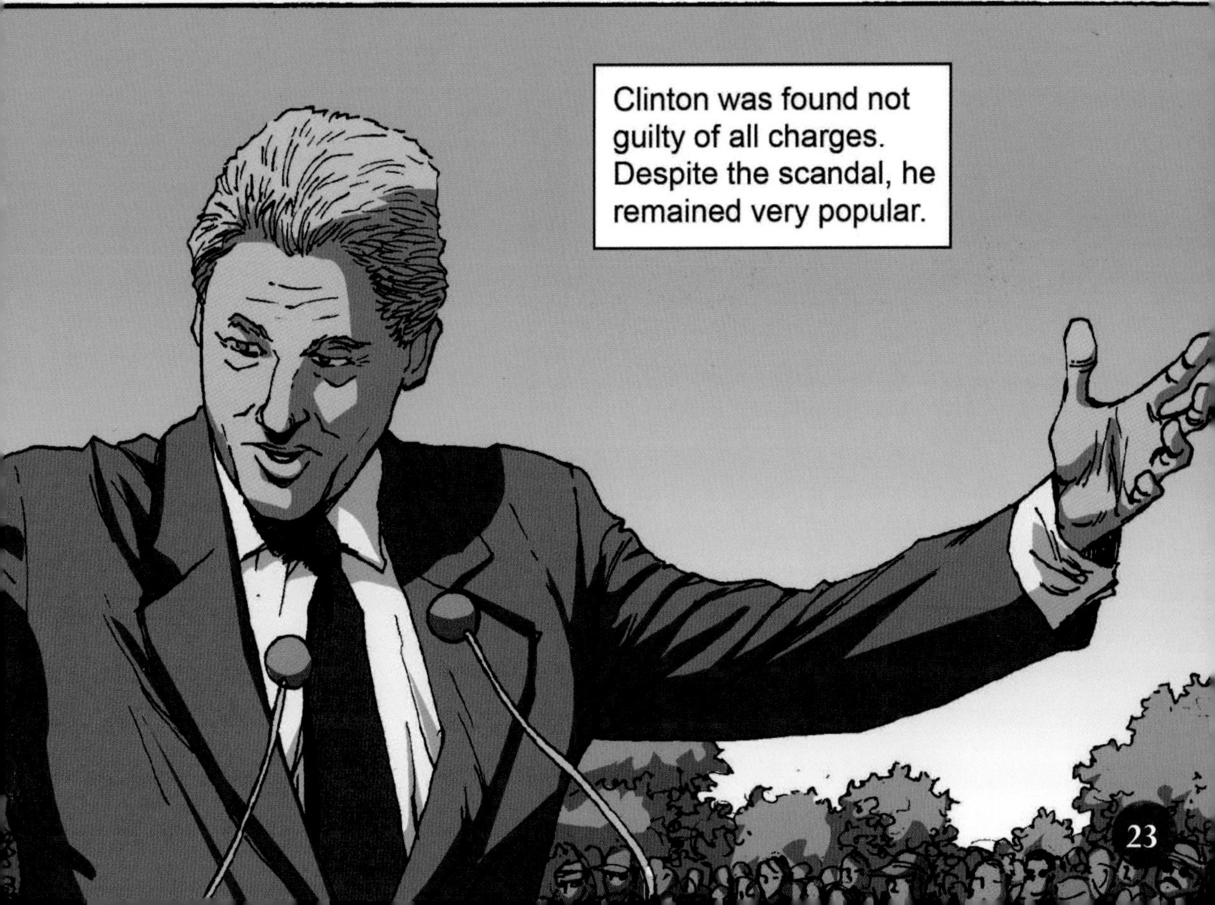
Clinton was found not guilty of all charges. Despite the scandal, he remained very popular.

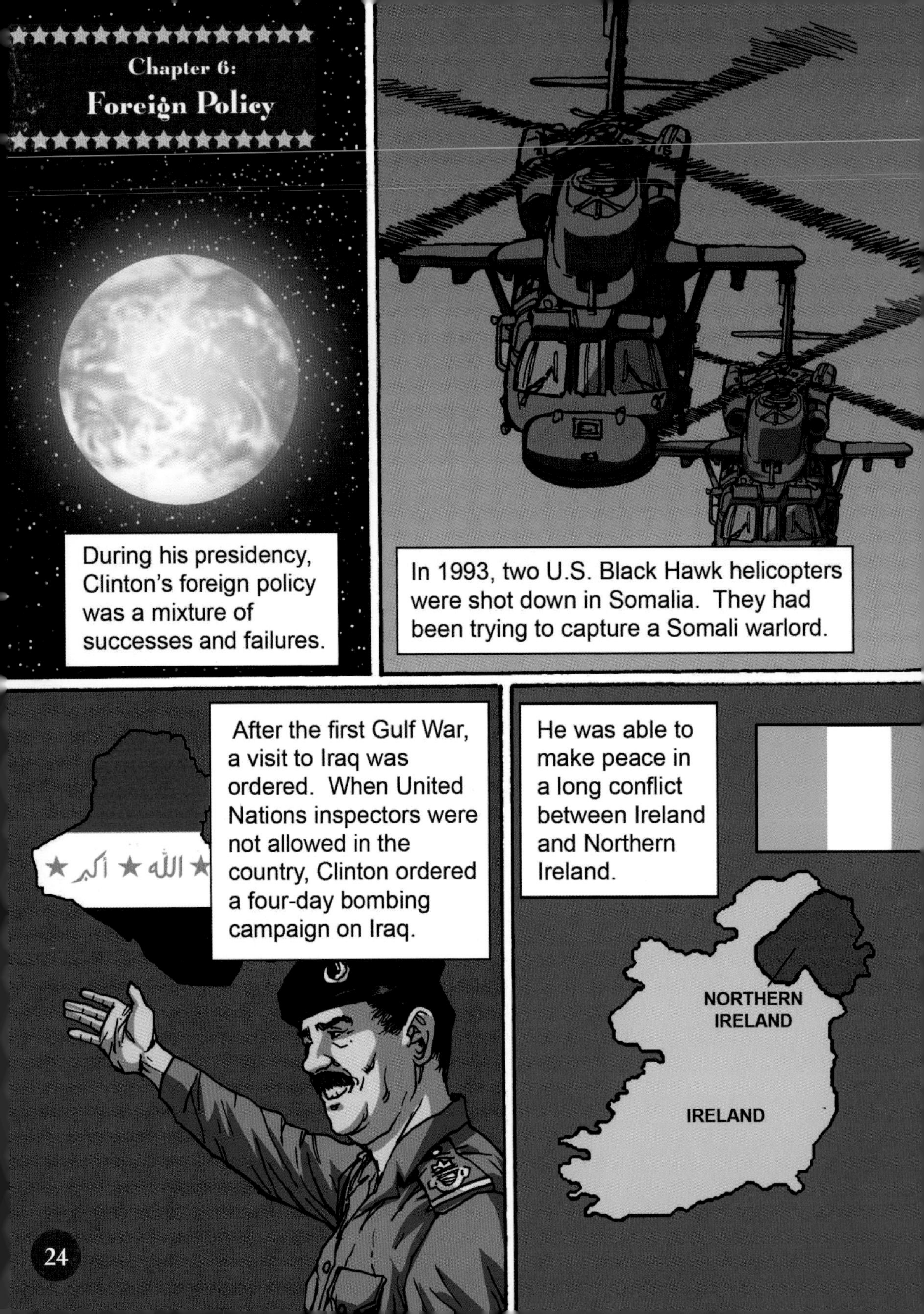
Chapter 6:
Foreign Policy
During his presidency, Clinton's foreign policy was a mixture of successes and failures.
In 1993, two U.S. Black Hawk helicopters were shot down in Somalia. They had been trying to capture a Somali warlord.
After the first Gulf War, a visit to Iraq was ordered. When United Nations inspectors were not allowed in the country, Clinton ordered a four-day bombing campaign on Iraq.
★ الله ★ أكبر ★
He was able to make peace in a long conflict between Ireland and Northern Ireland.
NORTHERN IRELAND
IRELAND

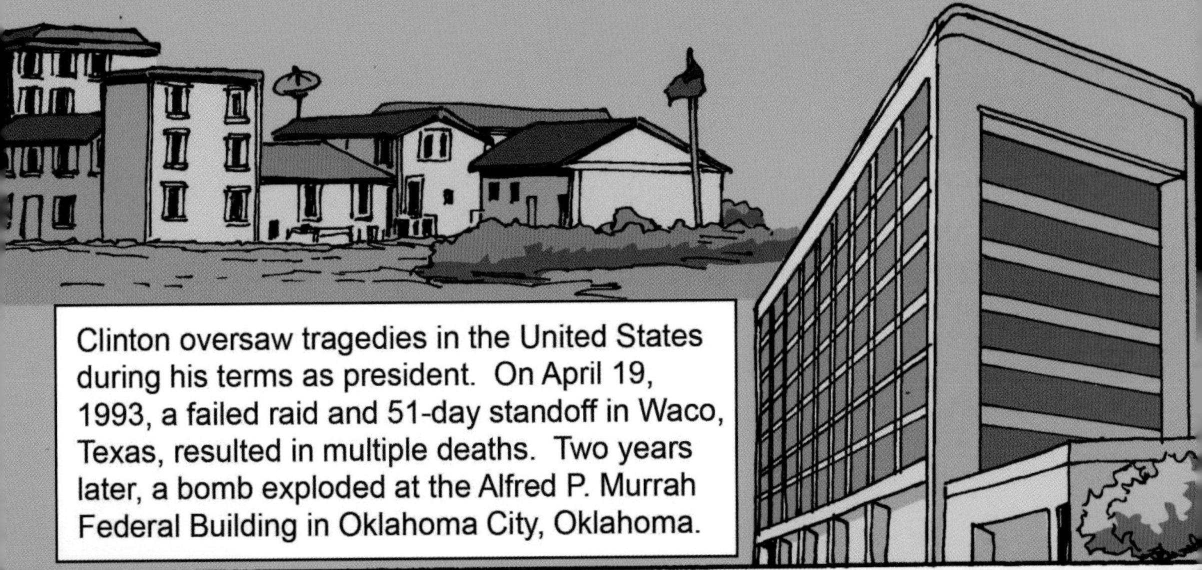
Clinton oversaw tragedies in the United States during his terms as president. On April 19, 1993, a failed raid and 51-day standoff in Waco, Texas, resulted in multiple deaths. Two years later, a bomb exploded at the Alfred P. Murrah Federal Building in Oklahoma City, Oklahoma.

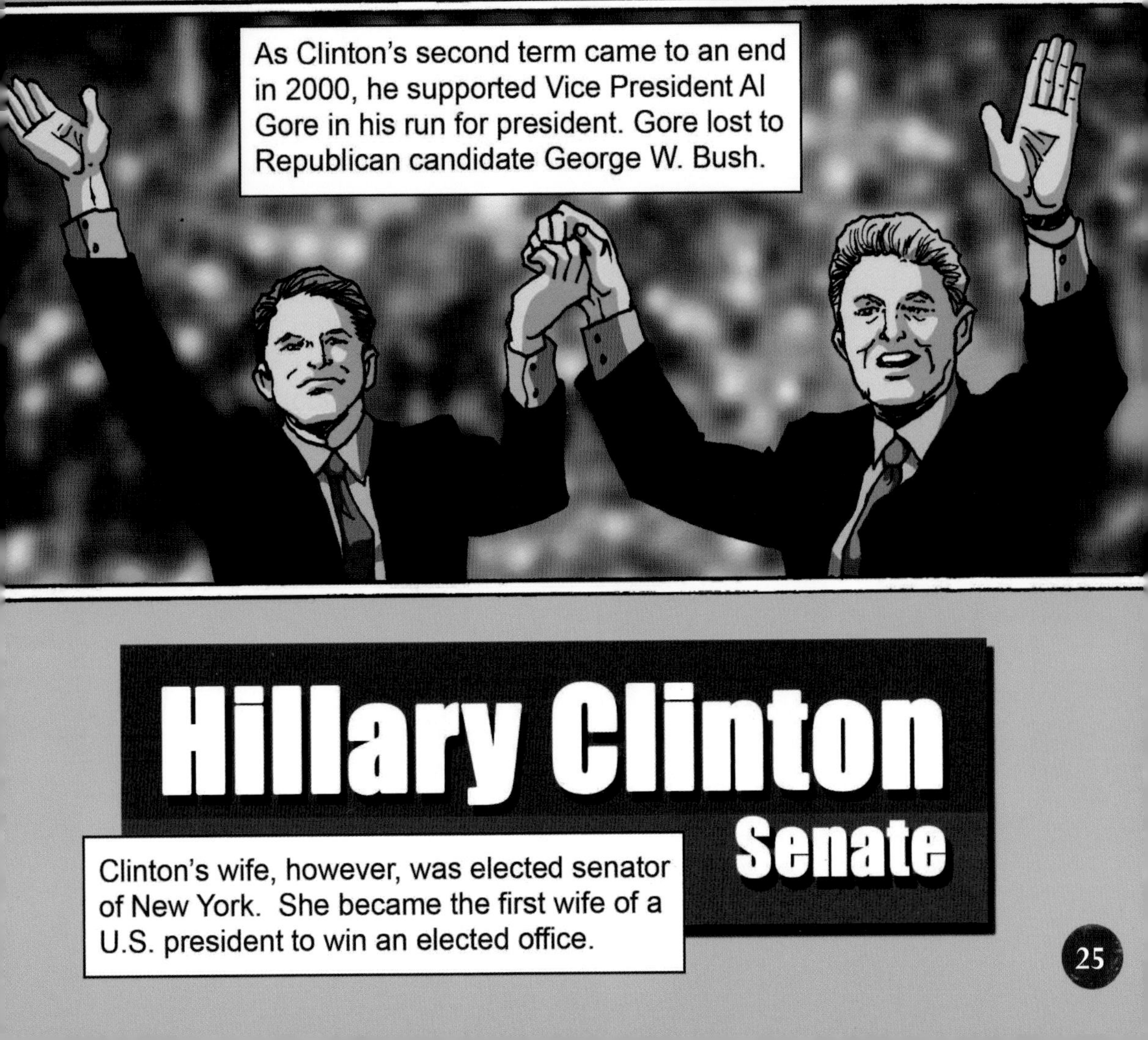
As Clinton's second term came to an end in 2000, he supported Vice President Al Gore in his run for president. Gore lost to Republican candidate George W. Bush.

Hillary Clinton

Senate

Clinton's wife, however, was elected senator of New York. She became the first wife of a U.S. president to win an elected office.

Chapter 7:
Retirement

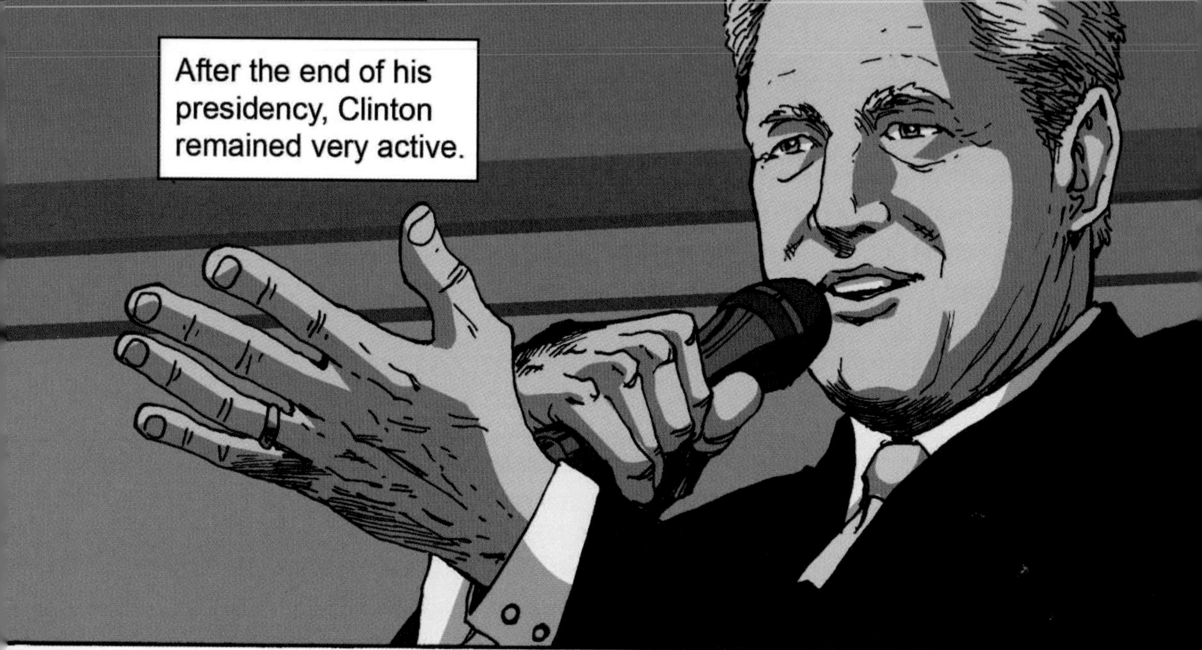
After the end of his presidency, Clinton remained very active.

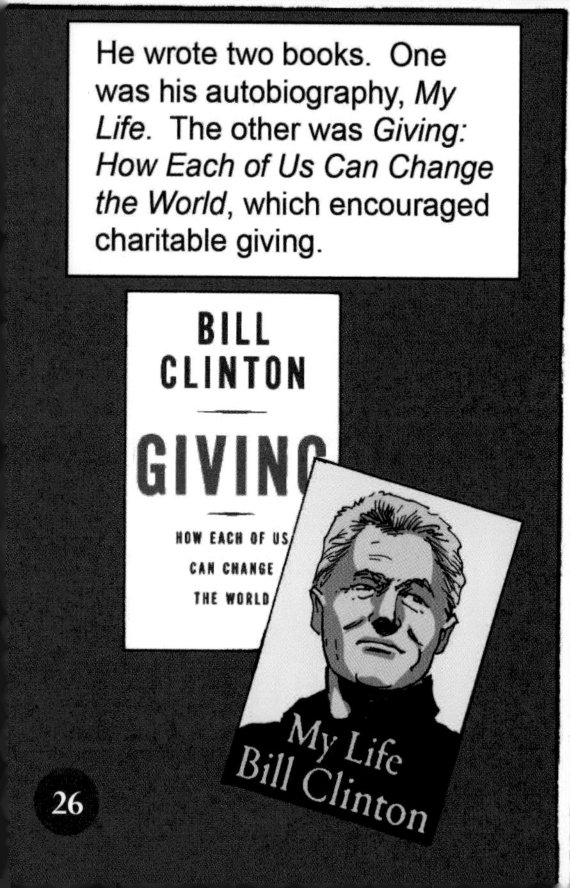
He wrote two books. One was his autobiography, *My Life*. The other was *Giving: How Each of Us Can Change the World*, which encouraged charitable giving.
BILL CLINTON
GIVING
HOW EACH OF US CAN CHANGE THE WORLD
My Life
Bill Clinton

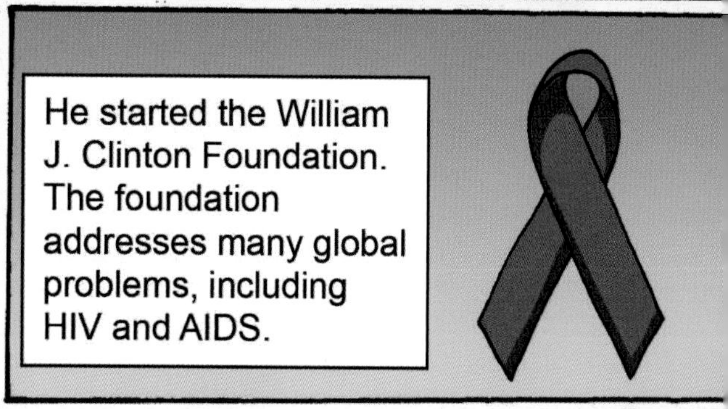
He started the William J. Clinton Foundation. The foundation addresses many global problems, including HIV and AIDS.

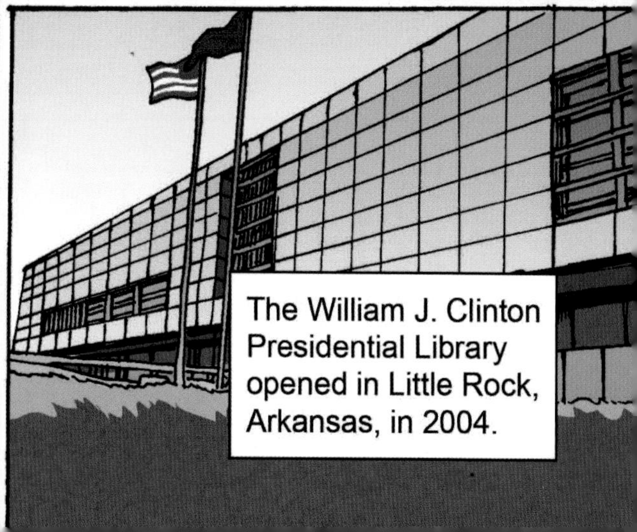
The William J. Clinton Presidential Library opened in Little Rock, Arkansas, in 2004.

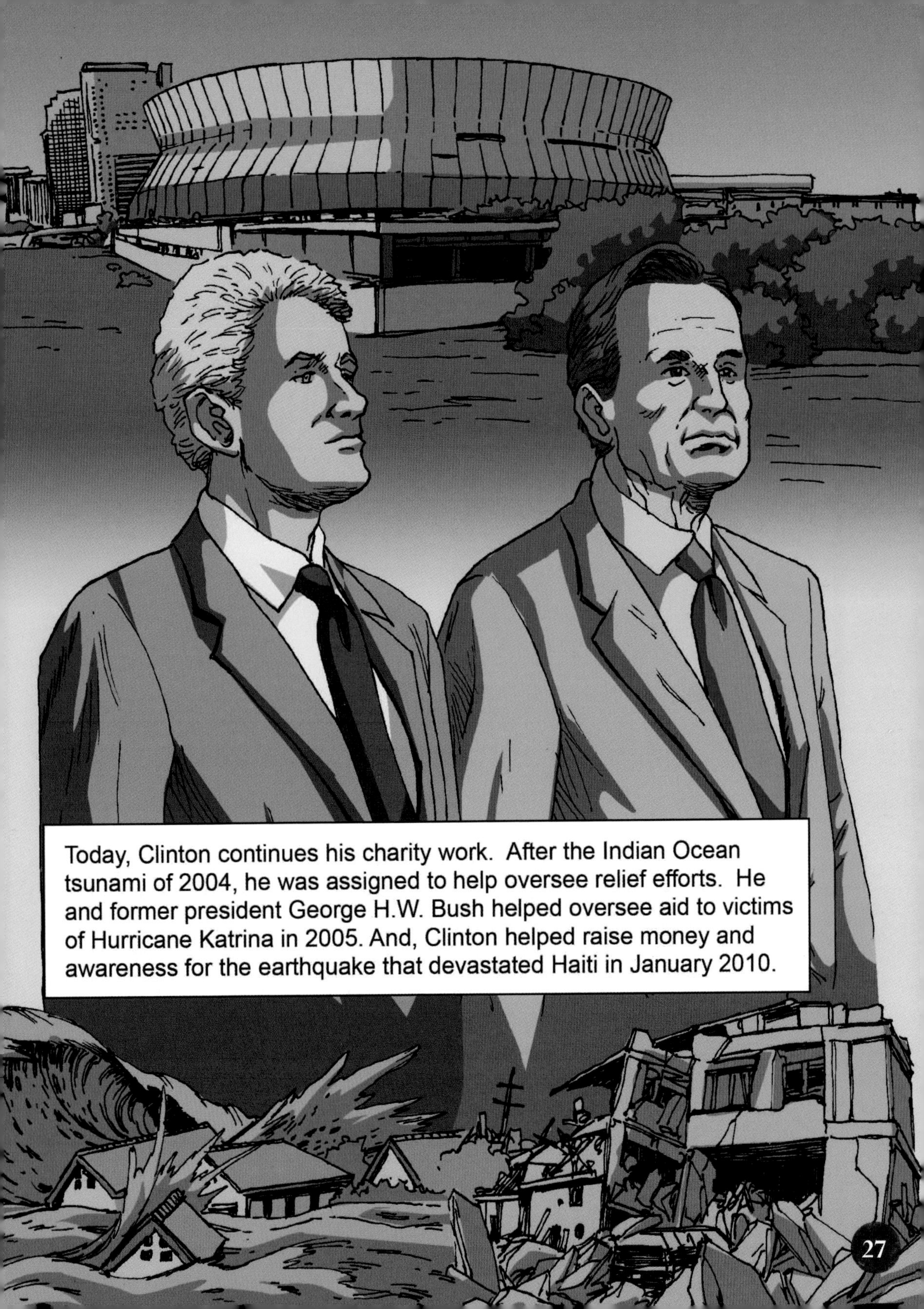
Today, Clinton continues his charity work. After the Indian Ocean tsunami of 2004, he was assigned to help oversee relief efforts. He and former president George H.W. Bush helped oversee aid to victims of Hurricane Katrina in 2005. And, Clinton helped raise money and awareness for the earthquake that devastated Haiti in January 2010.

Fast Facts

Name - William "Bill" Jefferson Clinton   Born - August 19, 1946
Wife - Hillary Rodham (1947–present)   Children - 1
Political Party - Democrat
Age at Inauguration - 46   Years Served - 1993–2001
Vice President - Al Gore

President Clinton's Cabinet

First term - January 20, 1993–January 20, 1997

- State – Warren M. Christopher

- Treasury – Lloyd Bentsen Jr., Robert E. Rubin (from January 10, 1995)

- Attorney General – Janet Reno

- Interior – Bruce Babbitt

- Agriculture – Mike Espy, Dan Glickman (from March 30, 1995)

- Commerce – Ronald H. Brown, Mickey Kantor (from April 12, 1996)

- Labor – Robert B. Reich

- Defense – Les Aspin, William J. Perry (from February 3, 1994)

- Health and Human Services – Donna E. Shalala

- Housing and Urban Development – Henry G. Cisneros

- Transportation – Federico Peña

- Energy – Hazel R. O'Leary

- Education – Richard W. Riley

- Veterans Affairs – Jesse Brown

Second term - January 20, 1997–January 20, 2001

- State – Madeleine Albright

- Treasury – Robert E. Rubin, Lawrence H. Summers (from July 2, 1999)

- Attorney General – Janet Reno

- Interior – Bruce Babbitt

- Agriculture – Dan Glickman

- Commerce – William M. Daley, Norman Mineta (from July 21, 2000)

- Labor – Alexis M. Herman

- Defense – William Cohen

- Health and Human Services – Donna E. Shalala

- Housing and Urban Development – Andrew M. Cuomo

- Transportation – Rodney Slater

- Energy – Federico Peña, Bill Richardson (from August 18, 1998)

- Education – Richard W. Riley

- Veterans Affairs – Togo D. West Jr., Hershel W. Gober (from July 25, 2000)

The Office of the President

- To be president, a person must meet three requirements. He or she must be at least 35 years old and a natural-born U.S. citizen. A candidate must also have lived in the United States for at least 14 years.

- The U.S. presidential election is an indirect election. Voters from each state elect representatives called electors for the Electoral College. The number of electors is based on population. Each elector pledges to cast their vote for the candidate who receives the highest number of popular votes in their state. A candidate must receive the majority of Electoral College votes to win.

- Each president may be elected to two four-year terms. The presidential election is held on the Tuesday after the first Monday in November. The president is sworn in on January 20 of the following year.

- While in office, the president receives a salary of $400,000 each year. He or she lives in the White House and has 24-hour Secret Service protection. When the president leaves office, he or she receives Secret Service protection for ten more years. He or she also receives a yearly pension of $191,300 and funding for office space, supplies, and staff.

Big Hollow Middle School
26051 W. Nippersink Rd.
Ingleside, IL 60041

Timeline

1946 - William "Bill" Jefferson Blythe was born on August 19.

1961 - Bill's last name was changed to Clinton.

1963 - Clinton visited Washington DC and met President Kennedy.

1968 - Clinton graduated from Georgetown University.

1973 - Clinton graduated from Yale University, taught at the University of Arkansas School of Law, and met Hillary Rodham.

1974 - Clinton ran for the U.S. House of Representatives but lost.

1975 - Clinton married Hillary Rodham.

1978 - Clinton defeated Lynn Lowe for governor of Arkansas and became one of the youngest governors elected.

1992 - Clinton got the Democratic nomination for president, selected Al Gore as running mate, and won the election.

1993 - Clinton was sworn in as the 42nd U.S. President on January 20.

1998 - Clinton was impeached for perjury and obstruction of justice, but was found not guilty.

2001 - Clinton established the William J. Clinton Foundation to address global problems.

2004 - Clinton released his autobiography, *My Life*; William J. Clinton Presidential Library opened in Little Rock.

2005 - Clinton was sent to help overseas relief efforts after the 2004 Indian Ocean tsunami. Clinton and George H.W. Bush helped oversee aid to victims of Hurricane Katrina.

2010 - Clinton oversaw aid to victims of the Haiti earthquake.

Web Sites

To learn more about Bill Clinton, visit ABDO Publishing Group online at **www.abdopublishing.com**. Web sites about Clinton are featured on our Book Links page. These links are routinely monitored and updated to provide the most current information available.

Glossary

Administration - the people who manage a presidential government.

campaign - to give speeches and state ideas in order to be voted into an elected office.

Democrat - a member of the Democratic political party. Democrats believe in social change and strong government.

Democratic National Convention - a national meeting held every four years. During the convention, the Democratic political party chooses its candidates for president and vice president.

electoral process - the process used to elect a U.S. president. The Electoral College is the group of representatives that elects the U.S. president and vice president by casting electoral votes. Each state has a certain number of representatives, or electors, based on population. Electors cast their votes for the candidate who received the most popular votes in their state.

grassroots movement - a political movement that grows through the actions of ordinary people.

impeach - to charge a public official for crime or misconduct in office.

intern - a student or graduate gaining guided practical experience in a professional field.

minority - a racial, religious, or political group that differs from a larger group in a population.

nomination - the act of choosing a candidate for election.

obstruction of justice - when a person interferes with the proper operations of a court or investigation by withholding information, lying, or hiding evidence.

perjury - the crime of telling a lie when under oath to tell the truth.

primary - a method of selecting candidates to run for public office. A political party holds an election among its own members. They select the party members who will represent it in the coming general election.

Republican - a member of the Republican political party. Republicans are conservative and believe in small government.

running mate - a candidate running for a lower-rank position on an election ticket, especially the candidate for vice president.

scandal - an action that shocks people and disgraces those connected with it.

surplus - an amount above what is needed.

Vietnam War - from 1957 to 1975. A long, failed attempt by the United States to stop North Vietnam from taking over South Vietnam.

Index